# James Pittar
## Swimming the Continents

by Claire Daniel
illustrated by Stephen Marchese

 Harcourt
SCHOOL PUBLISHERS

D1798504

Cover, ©Jamie MacDonald/Getty Images, ©Nick Servian/Alamy; 3, ©CORBIS; 5, ©AP Images; 6, ©Comstock/SuperStock; 7, ©Mark Dyball/Alamy; 8, ©Mark Dyball/Alamy; 9, ©Christopher Lee Lareus/Getty images; 10, ©Getty Images; 11, ©Patrick Ward/CORBIS; 13, ©David I. Moore/Alamy; 14,

Printed in China

ISBN 10:   0-15-377379-0
ISBN 13:   978-0-15-377379-2

Ordering Options
ISBN 10:   0-15-377149-6 (Grade 5 Collection)
ISBN 13:   978-0-15-377149-1 (Grade 5 Collection)
ISBN 10:   0-15-377861-X (package of 5)
ISBN 13:   978-0-15-377861-2 (package of 5)

2 3 4 5 6 7 8 9 10   0940   17 16 15 14 13 12 11 10 09

## A Big Challenge

The Cook Strait lies 17 miles (27.5 km) between the North and South Islands of New Zealand. Strong tides make swimming difficult. This channel beckons the most elite long-distance swimmers to challenge their physicality and determination in its water.

For Australian James Pittar, swimming the Cook Strait was a dream he would make a reality. He was an experienced swimmer. However, he faced a challenge beyond the Cook Strait. James had permanently lost his vision when he was a teenager. Not only was he going to swim the channel, but he was going to do so blind.

In 2005, James was set to swim the channel. Philip Rush, who had crossed the strait eight times, joined James's team and advised him on the challenge ahead.

Harsh weather creates impossible conditions so that the strait is impassable for many days out of the year. For eight days, Philip said the conditions were too harsh, and James unwillingly relented and did not begin. Finally, on March 5, Philip Rush said the magic words: "The swimming can begin."

James arrived at the starting point at South Island. His goal was to reach North Island. Once in the water, he immediately began swimming quickly, moving his arms more than sixty strokes per minute. He swam continuously. He only stopped to consume an energy drink or water, or to eat small snacks.

Carrying his supplies was a boat crew that followed James and helped guide his way. The crew devised a system of whistle blows to alert James of any direction changes he needed to make. One long whistle blow advised James that he should turn left. Two short blasts alerted James that he needed to veer right.

Map of New Zealand

When James was 492 feet (150 m) away from his goal, the crew could go no further because rocks threatened their safety. James would have to swim the last stretch alone because the boat crew could no longer follow him. This did not faze him. One member of his team, Chad Schneider, swam alongside James, continuing to whistle directions for him. After eight hours and twenty-nine minutes, in grueling conditions, James completed his swim. He became the forty-fifth person to finish the swim. However, he was the first blind person to ever complete such a feat.

## First Strokes

James Pittar was born on October 5, 1969. When he was eight years old, his family built a swimming pool in the backyard, and he would race with his father, brother, and sister. He enjoyed playing sports like cricket, rugby, and soccer. He also enjoyed playing chess and watching sports on television.

When James was fourteen years old, he was diagnosed with a rare eye condition. During the next two years, his ability to see clearly began to decline, until eventually he could no longer see. Many people would be infuriated with such a blow; however, James had a different approach. He did not become disheartened by his blindness. He loved to swim and was determined to swim with or without his sight.

James didn't want to just swim laps, though. He chose to attempt many of the toughest swimming challenges in the world. In 1998, he swam the English Channel. The 21.7 miles (35 km) of cold, choppy waters were some of the most daunting. James Pittar was the first blind person to swim across the channel.

That same year, James swam from Perth to Rottnest Island in Australia. He was the first blind swimmer to make the crossing. He went on to swim the crossing five more times by the year 2005.

In 1999, James swam the Manhattan Island Marathon Swim in New York City. He was the first blind swimmer to complete the 28-mile (45 km) course around the island of Manhattan.

In 2000, James tackled another huge challenge. He swam the Strait of Gibraltar from Spain to Morocco. James completed the 13.5-mile (22 km) swim, becoming the first Australian to swim from Europe to Africa. He was also the first blind person to complete the swim.

Tarifa Point, Strait of Gibraltar, Spain

James Pittar, above, finishes his swim to
Nantucket Island, Massachusetts

In the year 2000, James completed another daring
swim by covering the 16 miles (26 km) from Martha's
Vineyard to Nantucket Island in Massachusetts. He was
not only the first blind person to complete this swim—he
was one of the first two people ever to swim the stretch.

In 2003, he became the first blind swimmer to complete
three more major swims. He swam around Alcatraz
in San Francisco; he swam 4.35 miles (7 km) in the
Chesapeake Bay; and he swam 13 miles (21 km) from
Italy to Monaco.

Still, James had more ambitious plans in his mind. His
goal was to complete marathon swims in each continent
around the world. The Cook Strait was his first.

## Parana River Swim: June 2004

The next continent where James chose to swim was South America. The goal there was to swim 37.3 miles (60 km) on the Parana River in Argentina. He began the swim, which would take him from Puerto Gaboto to Rosario, on June 6, 2004.

Cold, strong currents and wind had been James's challenge in the Cook Strait. In the Parana River, he had another concern: barges.

The swim began at midday, around 11:20 a.m. The muddy water was choppy, and the water temperature was about 62° Fahrenheit (17°C).

At one point, a large barge was headed straight for James. James and his guiding kayak swerved to the side, making the swim longer and more difficult. The last ninety minutes, James swam in the dark, his body highlighted by a spotlight from a police boat. Finally, at 7:42 P.M., eight hours and twenty-two minutes later, the swim was completed.

A barge on the Parana River

## Swimming in South Africa

The next continent where James swam was Africa. He chose the Vaal River in South Africa. On March 26, 2005, the 15.5-mile (25 km) swim began. James predicted that the swim would take around eight hours; however, the course had different ideas. James had never

swum in fresh river water without currents like this. Still, even with a little trouble adjusting to the new water conditions, James was able to swim the river in only ten hours and forty-seven minutes.

## Swimming in Turkey

In September 2005, James swam along the Gallipoli peninsula in Turkey and into the Anzac Cove. With this swim, James marked another continent off his list—Europe.

Long-distance swimming is challenging for anyone. James says that one thing he does when the swim becomes difficult is to think of other things to take his mind off the swim. He says that sometimes he thinks of his wife, or of lying on his favorite beach in Sydney, or of jokes he has heard. When James is not swimming, he works in the Australian taxation office. When a swim is particularly difficult, he says that sometimes he even calculates taxes!

James swims for many reasons. He loves the feeling of being free and the openness of the water. He enjoys feeling the currents, tides, winds, and the waves crashing against him. Even the guiding whistle blows are comforting and exciting to him.

Bondi Beach, Sydney, Australia

As much as James has loved swimming for himself, many of his swims have been for others. In many of his swims, he has crusaded for people with disabilities or has raised money for worthy causes, including an organization that provides swimming and other activities for children with disabilities. In his six-continent challenge, James raised money for an organization that promotes eye health in Australia.

James doesn't consider his accomplishments eccentric or unusual by any standards. He simply made the best possible use of what he was given. He discovered that he thrives in the water and has shown the world that one doesn't need to see to achieve greatness.

# Think Critically

1. Why does James Pittar enjoy swimming for long distances all over the world?

2. What were some details of this story that were most interesting to you?

3. What do you think is the hardest thing that James Pittar has to do when he swims for long distances?

4. If you could ask James Pittar one question, what would it be?

5. What other person in real life does James Pittar remind you of?

 **Social Studies**

**Make a Map** Find and identify the seven continents of the world. Then use the dates and locations in the book to create a world map that shows where James Pittar swam and when.

 **School-Home Connection** Share with a family member James Pittar's milestones and achievements. Discuss what you learned reading about him.